This edition first published in 1997 by Lorenz Books

Lorenz Books is an imprint of Anness Publishing Limited
Hermes House, 88–89 Blackfriars Road, London SE1 8HA

This edition distributed in Canada by Raincoast Books, 8680 Cambie Street,
Vancouver, British Columbia V6P 6M9

ISBN 1-85967-865-3

A CIP catalogue record for this book is available from the British Library

Publisher: Joanna Lorenz
Managing Editor, Children's Books: Sue Grabham
Editor: Sophie Warne
Special Photography: John Freeman
Stylists: Isolde Sommerfeldt and Thomasina Smith
Design and Typesetting: Liz Black

The Publishers would like to thank Lindsay Porter and Ella Wilks-Harper for modelling for this book. Thanks also go to Jeff Abbott,
Brenda Marks and Keith Wilson.

Picture credits: Air France 15. Genesis 21bl. Papilio Photographic 7r, 3br, 13br, 19bl. Skyscan 10, 11tl, r and b,
17t and br, 19tr. Spacecharts 21tr. Tony Stone Worldwide 7bl. TRIP 9bl, 21br.
Zefa Pictures 5t and bl, 7tl, 8, 9tl and r, 13tr and c, 17bl, 19br, 23bl.

Printed in Hong Kong / China

1 3 5 7 9 10 8 6 4 2

LET'S LOOK AT
Flying
Machines

Nicola Tuxworth

LORENZ BOOKS

Jumbo jet

A jumbo jet has four powerful jet engines to lift it into the air.

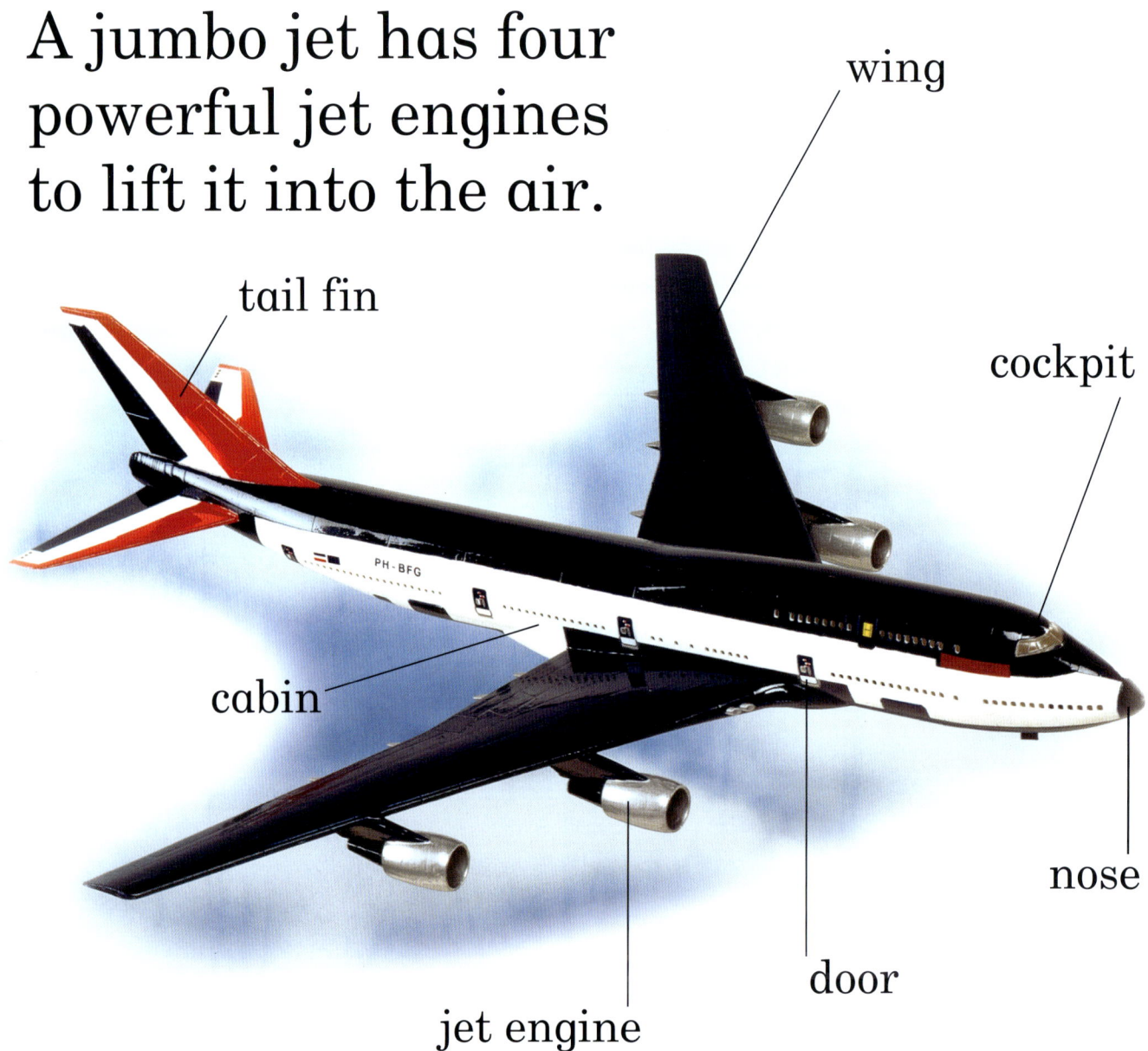

wing

cockpit

tail fin

cabin

nose

door

jet engine

Air traffic controllers tell the pilot which way to fly.

A jumbo jet needs lots of fuel to keep flying.

Planes fly people to countries all over the world.

Helicopter

A helicopter can fly backwards, forwards and sideways.

gearbox

tail rotor blade

main rotor blade

cockpit

830921

A helicopter can lift heavy loads.

A small patch of ground is big enough for a helicopter to land on.

Helicopters are sometimes used to rescue people.

Hot air balloon

A hot air balloon floats through the sky.

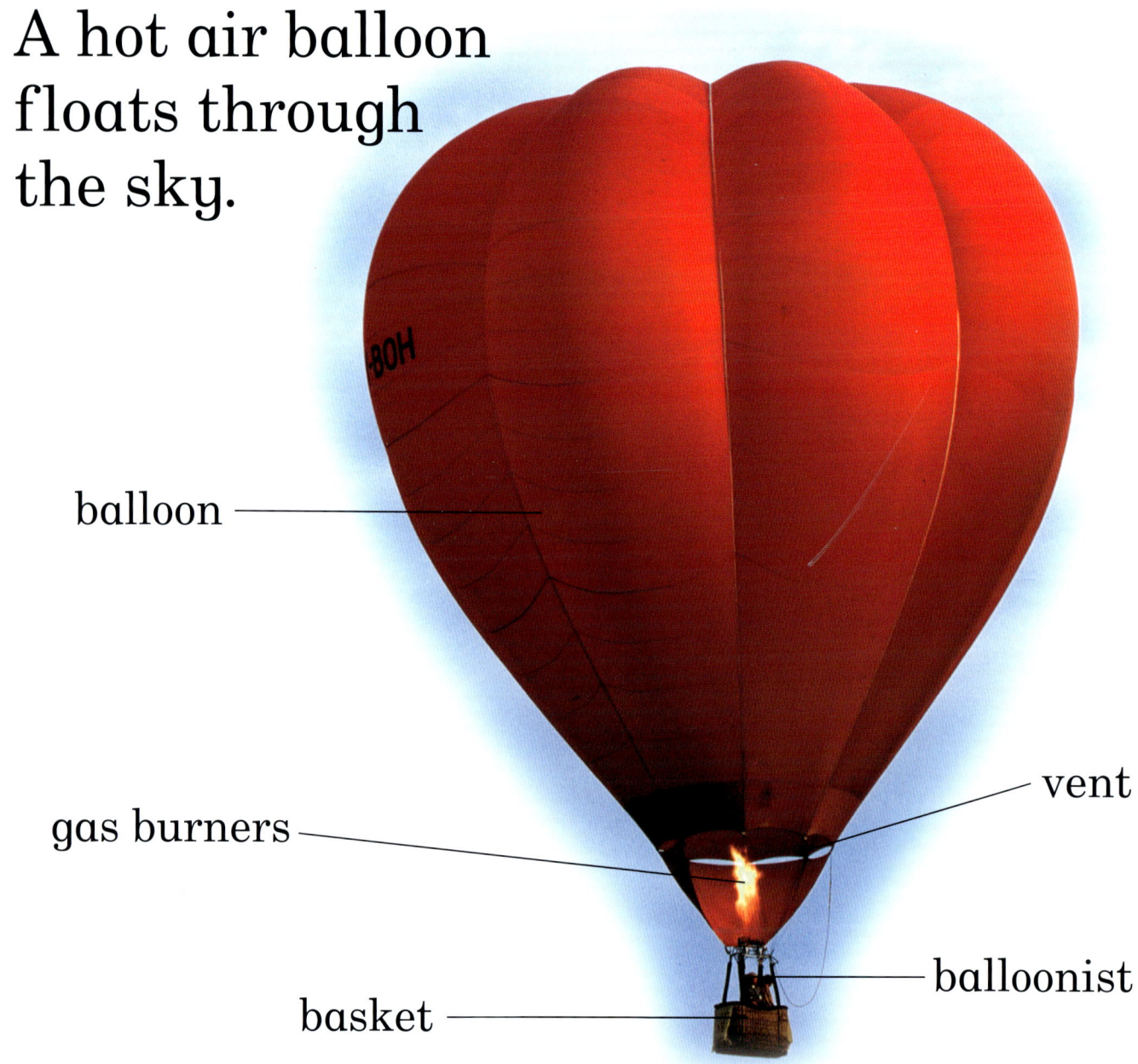

balloon

gas burners

vent

basket

balloonist

Gas burners heat the air in the balloon to lift it into the sky.

These balloons are racing each other.

Sometimes, tourists take a balloon trip to see herds of wild animals.

Hang-glider

A hang-glider uses wind power to lift one person up into the sky.

wing

pilot

main frame

control bar

pilot's body bag

Hang-glider pilots jump off high ground into the air.

To land safely, the pilot must steer carefully.

Hang-gliders can be packed up and taken to different places.

Seaplane

A seaplane can take
off and land on water.

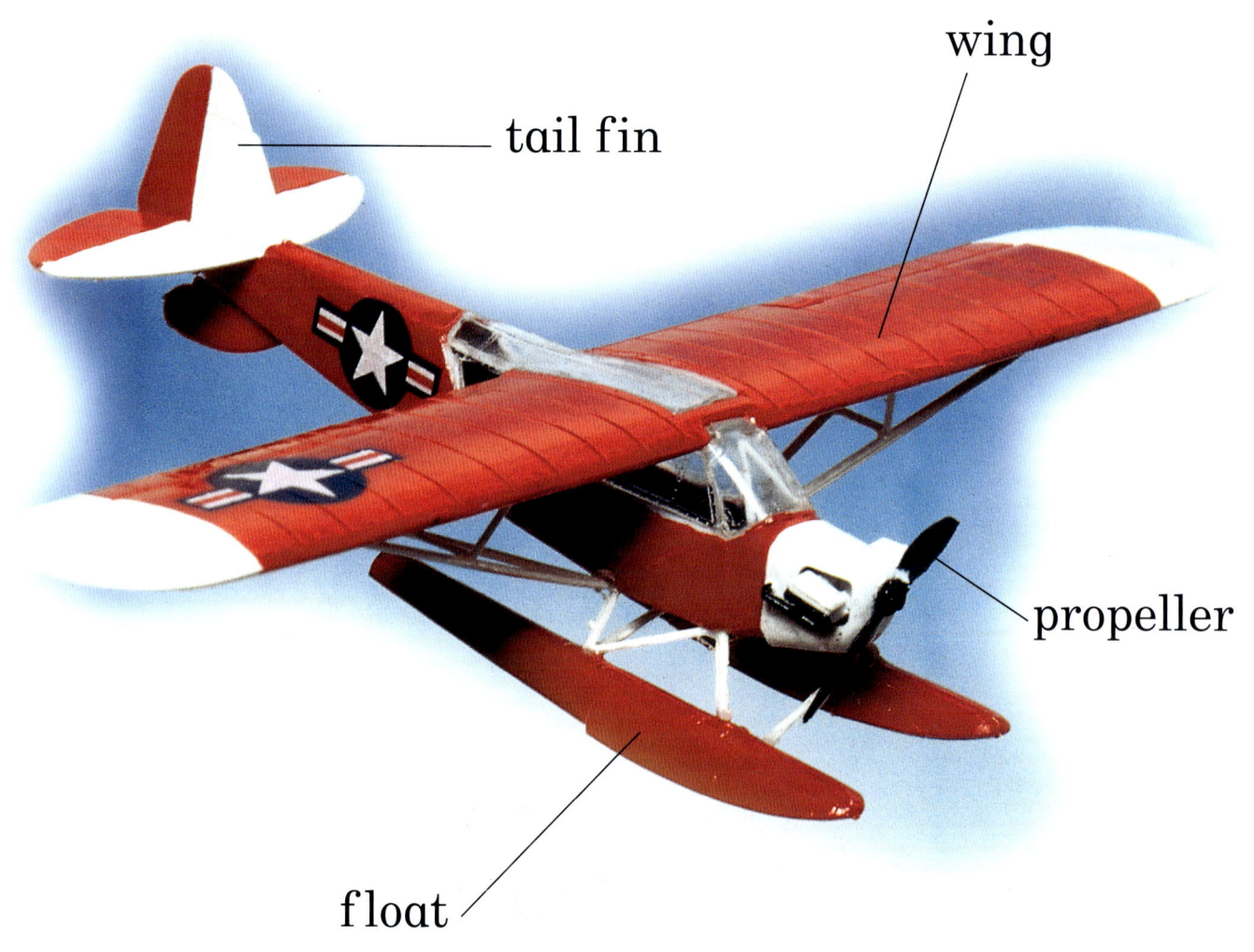

wing

tail fin

propeller

float

The wings are high up so they do not dip into the water.

A seaplane's powerful propellers make it fly.

Seaplanes fly nearer to the land than other planes.

Concorde

Concorde is the fastest
passenger plane in
the world.

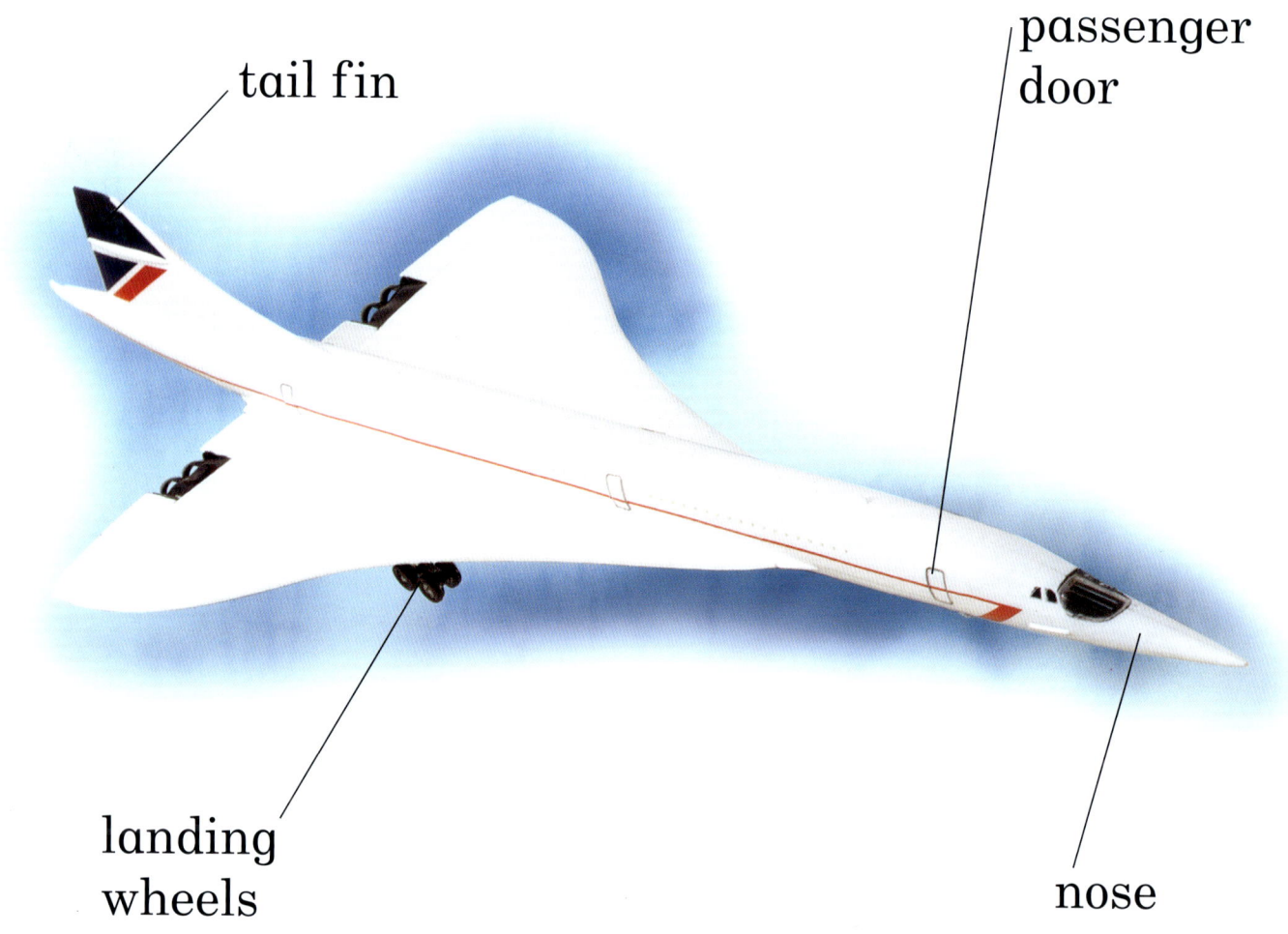

tail fin

passenger
door

landing
wheels

nose

Concorde can fly even faster than the speed of sound.

Concorde's nose is a special shape.

The nose can be tilted to help the pilot see more clearly.

Light aircraft

A light aircraft is a small plane. It can use a field or a beach as a runway.

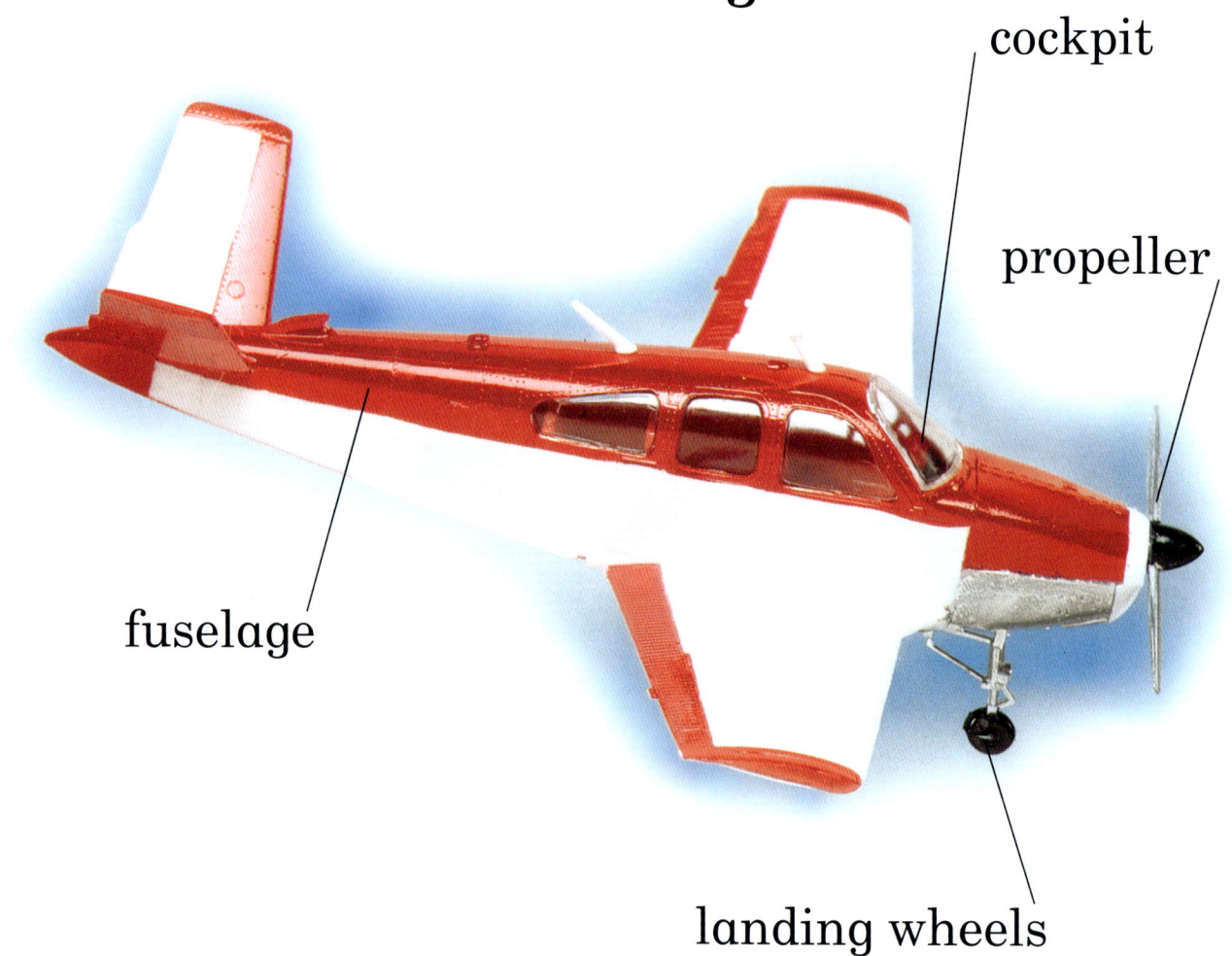

cockpit

propeller

fuselage

landing wheels

Pilots usually learn to fly in a light aircraft. A flying instructor teaches them what to do.

Some small airports are just for light aircraft. They are called airfields.

Light aircraft are used to spray chemicals on to crops.

Glider

A glider has no engine.
Its long wings help it to fly.

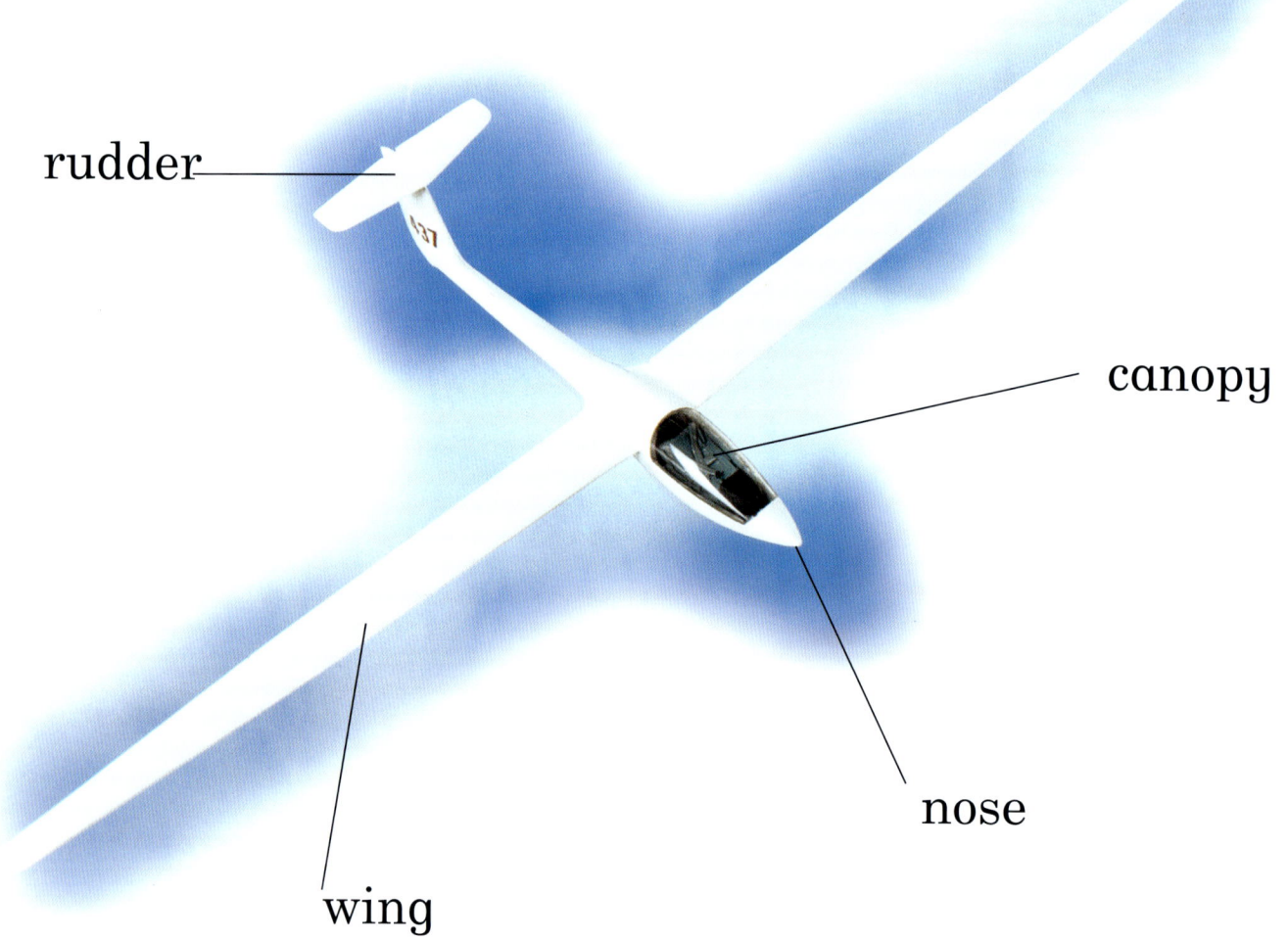

rudder

canopy

nose

wing

Gliders are towed
up into the sky.
They float gently
down to earth.

Birds can glide
through the
air too.

Sometimes
gliders can
fly for hours.

Space shuttle

A space shuttle is a rocket that glides through space.

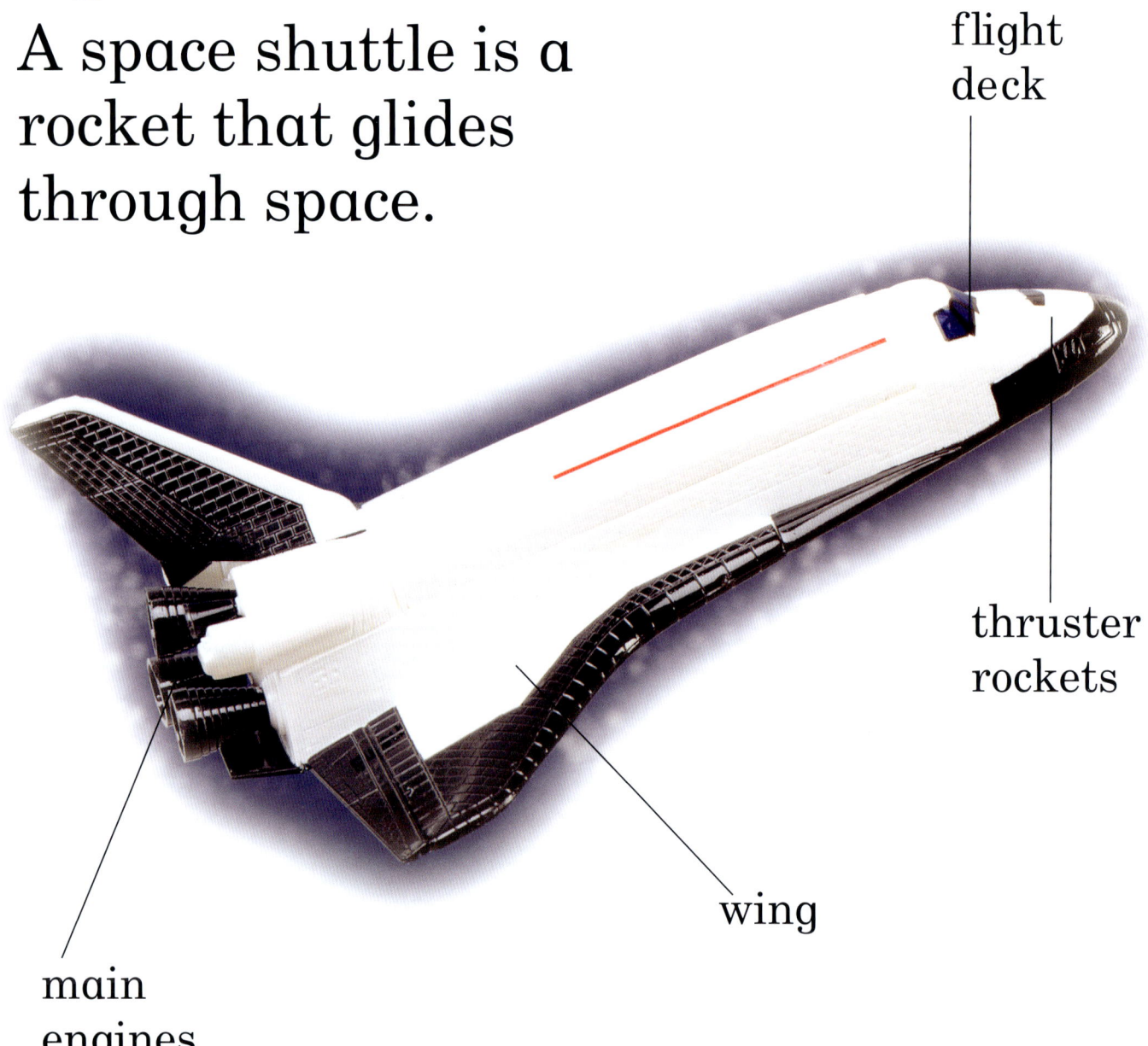

flight deck

thruster rockets

wing

main engines

Blaster rockets are used to launch a space shuttle.

Space shuttles land just like an ordinary plane.

Astronauts travel into space in a shuttle to mend broken satellites.

Name that flying machine!

Can you remember what all these flying machines are called?